Living the Marble Life

....

*A Weekly Exercise to Start Appreciating
Life One Moment at a Time*

DAVID G. BECKER

TURNING
STONE
PRESS

Cover design by Frame25 Productions
Cover art by Sylvie Corriveau c/o Shutterstock.com and
EpicStockMedia c/o Shutterstock.com

Turning Stone Press
8301 Broadway Street, Suite 219
San Antonio, TX 78209
www.turningstonepress.com

Library of Congress Control Number is
available upon request.

ISBN 978-1-61852-110-1

10 9 8 7 6 5 4 3 2 1

Printed in the United States of America

Contents

We spend so much time worrying about tomorrow, so little time appreciating today.

.

Acknowledgments

There are so many people who have contributed to the making of me, the inside and outside influences that molded me, the support system that shaped me, and the ultimate encouragement to write this book and to launch the parallel app. I would like to start with my mother, Joyce Becker—always the spiritual guide and sounding board, even when I wasn't feeling so spiritual. She always gave me the time to talk about me. Listening patiently and encouraging me to strive. I'd like to thank my father, Elliott Becker, who shaped my person and continues to talk to me from the stars. My sister, Caryn, for the good she brings to this world and who provided me with the seed from which this Life experiment grew. My sister Leslie for her poise, thoughtful approach, silent strength, playful childhood, and her ability and willingness to push everything aside to listen to her brother. And my sister Nicole, tackling every project with bubbling excitement and always expressing her pride in me while marching to her own entrepreneurial drum. My family has always displayed their internal support and has encouraged me to march to the beat of the day.

A special thanks to my beautiful daughter, Anika, who takes on much of my personality, wears her emotions on her sleeve, jumps up and down with excitement, and always smiles at the world. Prideful, giving, and the person I strive to be, she is always supporting Daddy and never questioning his intent or his often-wavering placements of thought.

I thank my son, Zachary, for his quiet confidence and his lack of interest in my shenanigans. He is smarter than he knows. Sensitive and confident and marching to his own music, he often teaches me that sensitivity and silence are a powerful pair.

And, of course, I'd like to thank my wife, Denise, who is always so supportive of my many projects and antics. Every project I take on is better because of her insights, artistic direction, laser focus, style, and cut-to-the-chase edits. I lean on her. While she doesn't always show it (she's not the jump-up-and-down type), she is always there for me, encouraging me to be me, as long as I don't make her too crazy in the process. She shows her approval without letting me get too big-headed about it . . . always keeping me level, grounded, humble, and laughing.

Lastly, I'd like to thank Murray, Aaron, Norman, and Cathy, old friends, with wisdom beyond my years, whose teachings continue to guide me through life. And let's not forget Banti. And the Dali Lama. And Rabbi Al. And the many authors, teachers, friends, and colleagues from whom I've learned and grown. And the *me*, that familiar voice so deep within that is always there, whispering to me, driving me forward in my life quest to be a better man.

Preface

I've always been fascinated by time. Not by the big chunks of time, but by the little moments that make up the big chunks of time. The moments that eat up the minutes that consume the day. The fleeting moments. Hours roll into days, days into weeks, weeks into years. Life slips by and we forget to savor the moment. We fail to seize meaning from the experience. Once the moment is gone, it is gone forever. We are already into the next moment. This deep-rooted existential philosophy drives us in our daily quest to better understand our true selves, to strengthen our interpersonal relationships, and to deepen the personal meaning of our life.

I knew for a long time I needed to develop a simple system to help me prioritize what is important in *my* life.

I developed Marble Life®, My Life Appreciation System®. It slows down time by encouraging me to focus on the little moments—the units of time that make up our body of life. This uniquely personal, symbolic, poignant, user-friendly Life Appreciation System provides a much-needed reminder during our daily routine that life is precious . . . and fleeting. That the people in our lives, and the experiences of the moment, are important in our search for true self.

There is one self-observation that has prompted me to develop My Life Appreciation System: Admittedly, I'm self-consumed. I always have been. I seldom make real time for others, including my loved ones, as I am so strongly focused on my many projects. I'm selfishly motivated. Because I'm so micro, I often struggle to see the bigger picture of life. *"Daddy, Daddy. Look at me."*

"In a minute, honey. I'm busy changing the world."

So, how do we slow down time, just long enough to appreciate the moment?

Read this book, download the app, and discover not just a Life Appreciation System, but an enlightening exercise you can immediately incorporate into your daily routine in your ongoing quest for self-discovery and life fulfillment.

Marble Life is a life tool, perfected through a decade of observation, experimentation, and practice. It will help you to become the person you want to be. It will keep you mindful, connected, and tethered to what is important in your life. It can be upgraded, downgraded, simplified, or modified. It grows with you. It can be opened or closed. It can be shared with friends and family or kept close to the heart as your symbol of soul. It is Marble Life, your personalized Life Appreciation System.

True to the colors that make you "*you*," Marble Life is your soulful sister and reminder that time is limited. Moments matter. You are in control of the details. And the outcome. Cradle the moment. Life's moments. Put life in perspective, approach life with vigor, and start to appreciate your life and the people in it.

Life appreciation starts today!

Introduction

I was seven years old when I built an indoor tent with my sister, Leslie, out of a frayed, yellow blanket, propped up by draping the corners of the blanket across the backs of the bedroom chairs. We would huddle under the tent for hours and pretend. It was then when I invented, or should I say discovered, electricity. I would drag my fingers across the blanket, and yellow sparks would dance from my fingertips. Wow, was I excited. I'm not sure when exactly I learned that my discovery was static electricity.

When I was a little boy, I was fascinated by my little discoveries. One of those discoveries that I was intrigued by was time. I loved watches and sundials and old people. I always wondered how I could package time. Or invent a tool to help people appreciate the time in their day and to parcel out moments of time based on their priorities.

Years later, in college, I took a course in philosophy. It was fascinating. What was intended to be an easy elective turned out to be one of the most challenging classes of the semester. It opened my mind. While we studied the great philosophers, the one thing that stood out, that resonated with me, was the theory of existentialism. As deceptively simple as the concept was, it was difficult for me to grasp and nearly impossible to explain, with any clarity, to another person. I remember trying to explain it to my mother. It was a short-lived conversation. What I do remember, though, was its impact on me. I learned that existentialism was about the moment we are living in. Once that moment passes, it is gone, as we are already into the next moment. You cannot get that moment back.

One day, when I went home for the weekend from college, I found a Buddhist monk living in my bedroom. To say that was weird would be a vast understatement. What was this monk doing living in my room? He was wrapped in a baggy brown robe. With a hood (the first hoodie, I suppose). He was quiet and wise beyond his years. Beyond my years. He walked, and talked, with purpose. My mother, Joyce, invited him to live with us for a short time. And to speak to her group of friends about life and his spiritual beliefs and worldly experiences. He would talk about life and living and the power of silence. And listening. And observation. His name was Banti.

It wasn't until many years later, when I traveled to Sri Lanka for an importing project, to the ancient Dambulla Rock Temple, a sacred learning ground of the Buddhist monk, that I searched for Banti. I climbed the steep, dusty steps up the mountain, with monkeys piercing at me from the sides of the climb. When I arrived at the temple, a temple complex dating back to the first century BC, and walked into the deep, cool, open cavern (one of five caves under a vast, overhanging rock) to view the giant sleeping Buddha, I approached a senior monk and asked him if he knew Banti. He looked at me with peaceful eyes and whispered, with purpose, "We are all Banti."

Then, in 2002, my sister forwarded me a story that was bouncing around the Internet. This article, anonymous at the time, was based on *1,000 Marbles: A Little Something about Precious Time* by Jeffrey Davis, in which the main character calculates that he has approximately 1,000 Saturdays left in his life, and that each one beyond those 1,000 Saturdays was a special gift. It inspired me and changed my life. That inspiration prompted me to incorporate a simple exercise into my weekly routine, one that I followed religiously for the next thirteen years, and counting. The philosophy and physicality behind that routine, coupled with my observations and experiences, serve as the foundation for my physical and virtual exercise. It falls under the broad category of Self-Improvement, yet propels far beyond Self-Help, establishing a new genre I call "Life Appreciation."

Marble Life is a unique, daily, immersive, visual, entertaining, soul-strengthening Life Appreciation System that is designed to help you live each moment in the now, by being fully present with the moment you are living in by using a physical object as a representation of a certain increment of time. By carrying this object with you, you will be reminded to live in the current moment—since you can never get it back once it has passed. This exercise is simple and powerful, and you carry it in your pocket. I anticipate Marble Life will shake up your world as it has mine, strengthen the human existence, and organically gain international acclaim—one monumental marble at a time.

Somewhere along the line, I realized I needed to share Marble Life with the world. This book will help you to understand the Marble Life Appreciation System and to implement it in your daily life to bring more awareness to each moment in it.

Join me through my personal journey of self-discovery, observation, and a mindful expedition that started out as a fun little experiment and grew into a lifelong exercise of self-awareness. Follow along as I dissect my thinking and share the emotions I experienced and the learnings I amassed. I hope that my discoveries will help you to look deep within yourself.

⇐ 1 ⇒

Growing Up

GROWING UP, I WAS ALWAYS BUSY. When I was a little kid, we'd play Kick the Can, Freeze Tag, and Curb Ball with a vengeance, in the street with the local neighborhood kids until the sun went down and darkness fell over our concocted playground. When I grew a little older, I learned that I could make money with odd jobs, including a paper route, sweeping the floor in a local salon, working retail, flipping burgers, performing magic, and helping my mother with her various businesses. As I grew even older, into young adulthood, there was always a business I wanted to start or a product I wanted to invent. I was intense. I had big lofty dreams. There were lots of projects and businesses. That's the subject for another book.

Time marched on. I started a family.

My daughter, when she was little, would always ask me to read her a story in bed. I would climb into her little white brass-piped Charles Rogers bed and read to her, because that's what dads are supposed to do. And because

I wanted to have a different relationship with my daughter from the one I had had with my father. I wanted to know her. And I wanted her to know me. To really know me. That was the conscious me. The unconscious me was buried in my work and whatever project I was working on at the time. I began to notice a trend. A trend I wasn't happy about. My daughter, Anika, would walk into my small guest-room office and ask me to read to her. Or talk to her. Or listen to her. Or play with her. But I was so wrapped up in my project, in my thoughts, in myself, in my life, that I didn't make the time. *"In a minute, honey. I'm busy changing the world."*

This is about the time when my older sister, Caryn, shared with me that email about *1,000 Marbles*. The main character in that story determines that he has only a set number of Saturdays left in his life—1,000 to be exact—and to mark each Saturday, he goes out and buys a jar of 1,000 marbles. He takes one marble out of the jar each Saturday to show the passage of time. After all 1,000 marbles are gone, he begins to recognize each following Saturday as a special gift, a little extra time, and something to be cherished.

It was like catching a punch square on the chin. At that moment, my life changed.

Awakening

MY FATHER, ELLIOTT ROBERT BECKER, born in 1926 in Brooklyn, New York, and a product of the Great Depression, was a good-looking man, as a young adult and as a senior. People said he looked like Ernest Hemingway. And he did. The resemblance was remarkable. He loved to dance. And play chess. And chart the stock market. After high school, he joined the Navy, where he served his country in World War II. I learned that he wanted to be a salesman. Hard for me to believe. He always seemed like the accountant that he became. I don't know if he was happy. I don't remember hearing him laugh.

My father died when he was seventy-three years old, on a cruise ship off the coast of Nice, dancing and eating and playing chess. He was the sweetest, smartest, most humble person I have ever known. I strive to be like him (but I often come up short). His mother, Frieda, was tough. An old-school disciplinarian. She would teach and rule by the belt, as my Grandfather Abraham (they called him Al) would sit silent. Grandpa Al owned candy stores in

Brooklyn. They moved often. He was a round man with a twinkle in his eye and a crooked smile. He didn't say much. My father loved him and often said he was the sweetest, most humble person he had ever known. But my father never really got to know him. Grandpa Al died when he was seventy-three.

My father died when he was seventy-three years old. My grandpa Al also died when he was seventy-three years old.

Now, here I was, forty years old. I thought of my father. And his father. And my mother. And my daughter. And my son. And my wife. And my sisters. And all of the moments in my life that I will never get back.

I took pen to paper and wrote a simple math problem. Seventy-three years minus forty years equals thirty-three years. Thirty-three years at fifty-two weeks equals 1,716 marbles. That's 1,716 weeks before my seventy-third birthday. I wanted to find a way to visually represent these 1,716 weeks until my seventy-third year, when I would be the same age as both my grandfather and my father when they passed. My thinking was profound. I jumped in my car, ran to a local arts and crafts store, and set out to find 1,716 marbles in different colors and sizes and textures. I also bought a big glass vase.

I raced home and scooped up my five-year-old daughter. We dumped all of the marbles on the carpeted floor and started to count them into piles of ten. We gathered ten piles of ten and pushed the small piles into larger piles of one hundred. We carefully, and I mean really carefully, counted, and then recounted, 1,716 marbles. The marbles of my life. I didn't want to get the count wrong (this is my life we are talking about). We then slowly rolled the marbles into the tilted glass vase, and then dropped them, one by one, marble by marble, pile by pile, clank by clank, into the vase until the 1,716th marble was resting comfortably atop a pile of wildly assorted colored marbles. My project was complete. I carried the marble-filled vase into the bowels of my bedroom closet, shimmied it across the carpet until it rested comfortably, peacefully, in its private, personal space. The marbles of my life, waiting to be spent.

This is where my spiritual journey took a 180-degree turn from the marble story my sister shared with me a few years earlier. In the story she shared, you were supposed to take out a marble every week with the purpose of watching the level of marbles slowly diminish, as in the days of our lives, so that you would see that any time over the allotted amount would be a gift. Instead, rather than focusing on the remaining, unspent marbles sitting idle in my jar of life, my mind focused, fixated, on the single selected marble, the marble of the moment, so that I could honor *each* moment as a gift, not just the ones above and beyond what I had calculated.

How I would choose to spend my first marble, and every marble in my jar of life, would ultimately define me, set my Life Appreciation System into motion, and shade and color the days of my life and the wide-ranging experiences that would make up my life.

My exercise was simple. Every Saturday morning for the next thirteen years and counting, I would religiously— or should I say spiritually, or maybe we'll just go with consciously—walk into my bedroom closet and blindly reach into my glass vase and pull out a single marble. I would look at it, roll it across my fingers, feel its weight, admire its beauty, give it a kiss, and project onto my marble who I wanted to be and what I wanted to accomplish this week. I would then place this very special marble into my right pocket.

Throughout the day and the ensuing week, I would hold my marble, marvel at my marble, roll my marble, interact with my marble, project on my marble, reflect on my marble, internalize my marble, and recognize its existence and its correlation to this exact, right-here-and-now moment in my life.

Every Friday (before my Saturday morning ritual), I would discard my marble. I would toss it away. Throw it out . . . as that moment of time had passed. I would drop the used marble into the trash; throw it into the river; fling it onto the fairway; drop it into the street sewer; bounce it off the sidewalk; heave it into the trees; kick it into the leaves; flick it into nowhere; or just give it away. The discarding of my marble was just as profound as its selection . . . maybe even more so. Saturday morning, first thing, I would go through the same exercise.

A new marble! A new day! A new experience!

Marble Life— The Object of Your Desire

ACCORDING TO WIKIPEDIA, AN OBJECT (*something*—some of *Everything*, the *face of it)* is a technical term in (modern) philosophy often used in contrast to the term *subject*. A subject is an observer and an object is a thing observed.

So, for this example, we are the observer of our life.

An object is anything we can think about, touch, or talk about. It is an entity, like a pyramid, an apple, a shoe, a stone, or a marble. An object refers to any definite being or thing. One approach to defining an object is in terms of the object's properties and its relation in the universe to other things, such as its color, its weight, its size, its dimension. An object can be big or round. Black or blue. Opaque or transparent. Heavy or light. Smooth or textured. But where that object sits in relation to your life, or your perception of your life, is where it gets interesting.

Marble Life

For Marble Life, we select a small object that represents a specified unit of time. Your object can be a pebble, a token, a paper clip, a coin, or whatever object suits your fancy. Personally, I use a marble, which is why I call this exercise Marble Life. It could represent one weekend; one Saturday, one week, one month. Your unit of time is up to you. We carry that object, that symbolic unit of time, close to our body, as a physical/virtual reminder that life during that specified time frame is what we make of it. After that unit of time expires (e.g., the week passes), we discard the object. We throw it away. It serves as a powerful reminder that that object, that moment, that single unit of time, is gone—forever. It reminds us to place more emphasis on the moment.

Why a Marble?

A marble is a clean slate. An island. An entity unto itself. Beautiful, simple, rich in tradition, tactile, and smooth to the touch. A marble is easy on the eye. And the wallet. A collection of color. A blank canvas from which to express, explore, and project. Easy to acquire and fun to collect, a marble is affordable. Or rare and expensive. It can be plain or artistic. Or expressive. Clear or exploding with personality. It whispers one word. Or screams a statement. You can roll it. Spin it. Play with it. Trade it. You can get lost in its shine and perplexed by its inner beauty. There is something about a marble . . .

A marble can be lots of things to lots of people.

A marble is:

- Peaceful
- Pure
- Perfect
- Simple
- Substantive
- Sensual
- Spiritual
- Stable
- Reflective
- Tranquil
- Fluid
- Beautiful
- Bountiful
- Calm
- Motionless
- Endless
- Powerful
- Something
- Nothing

Why a marble? I choose to use a marble as my object because it is small and fits easily into my pocket. But beyond its tiny size, I find that a marble possesses the alluring properties and qualities I've listed above. These qualities live in my mind and are projected onto my marble as it travels with me throughout my day. I can get lost in a marble. And I do. To me, it's my little secret. Having it sitting in my pocket, acutely aware of its presence, I can roll a marble between my fingers and connect on a deeper level. It has meditative qualities. Rolling my marble is relaxing and helps me to look within. I find a marble unassuming yet powerful. The colors of marbles are often beautiful and vibrant. Or muted and simple. The colors and patterns are as diverse as the stars in the sky and as textured as my day. A marble works for me. You can choose any object that works for you. Your object can be half dollars. Every week you give one away. Or a ball of seeds, tossed away to grow wherever it lands. Your object can be a paper clip, a penny, or a bottle cap. Of course, any object will do, as long as it resonates with you.

Channeling Your Object

While your Marble Life marble is beautiful in its raw form, it is only an object until you give that object meaning and purpose. Your weekly marble is about harnessing the tremendous power that you possess, a power that lies deep within your subconscious mind and within the confines of your inner being. Marble Life is about channeling or projecting your thoughts, your desires, your wants, and your focus to one object. That object, in this case your Marble Life marble, is no longer an inanimate object, but a reference point that is powered by your energy. Now, every time you feel or touch or sense your marble, you are not simply feeling an object but everything that that

object now stands for. That marble is you. It is today—
it is the very real, right-now moment in your life. That
marble represents all that your life has to offer . . . and
all that you have to offer your life. That marble is you.
Today. Now.

I call this projection channeling. Without projection
channeling, all of your thoughts come and go in and out
of the ether. It is not only hard, it is nearly impossible,
to gather your thoughts, hold onto them, sort them into
any meaningful priority, and channel them if you don't
have a symbolic, physical something to channel them to.
Once you are able to project, or channel, your thoughts,
desires, wants, and goals to your object, your object takes
on meaning and serves as a physical reference point, a
landing sphere, a forceful (or should I say force field)
reminder of your channeled energies. If your desires are
floating around, without a special something to capture
your projected channeling, you will not be able to fully
harness your power of thought. Your marble is your con-
duit to action . . . the change you seek in yourself.

When you carry around your marble for the week, you
are carrying around everything that your marble stands
for. When you finally toss your marble, you are releasing
yourself—and allowing yourself to be free and to grow to
the new you of the moment.

Simply Marvel at Your Marble—or Go Deeper

Each day you can simply marvel at your marble. Your
marble is your visual reminder. It is for you and you only.

Your marble sits in your pocket. Or on your person. Or on your home screen. It can twirl. Bounce. Spin. Stand tall. Stand still. Or just be. What you choose to do with your marble (or your object of choice), and how you opt to interact with your marble, are entirely up to you.

❧ 4 ❧

Psychology behind Marble Life

Selection. Projection. Reflection.
Ejection. (Repeat.)

THERE IS A FORCE BEHIND MARBLE LIFE. And you are the source of that powerful force. A force field created by the subject and projected onto the object. The stronger your belief in the exercise, the deeper your commitment, the bigger the force field, the greater the results.

I have been participating in the same Marble Life exercise, nearly religiously, for over a decade (as of this writing). What keeps it fresh? What keeps me coming back for more, with a passion that is stronger than the week prior? Good question. And a question that I never thought of, nor did I have an answer to, until recently. There is an emotional tie, a psychological draw, to the mindful exercise of the Marble Life program that keeps me coming back and keeps me invigorated and engaged from moment to moment . . . and week to week . . . and year to year. I'm in my thirteenth year and counting. I haven't missed a day. Or a week. This is not by accident.

At one point, recently, and at the suggestion of some colleagues, I looked to replicate my physical Marble Life exercise into a virtual one, marrying the two realms. During this period of exploration and discovery, I was asked by a member of my app-development team to think long and hard about the emotions that run through my mind, day to day, week to week, throughout my physical Marble Life exercise process. Interesting thought and quite insightful. No one had ever asked me that question before. They wanted to know because they wanted to capture, and mirror, those raw emotions that keep me coming back for more during my physical exercise routine. They wanted to define those emotions, replicate them, and then incorporate them into a virtual Marble Life exercise, one that parallels my physical version. After much thought and some probing around my psyche, I identified the process of Selection; Projection; Reflection; Ejection; (Repeat), and the four raw emotions that run through my mind on a weekly basis. They are, in exact order:

1. Anticipation

2. Excitement

3. Introspection

4. My unwillingness to let go

Let me break this out for you.

Selection = Anticipation.

Every Saturday morning, when I walk into my bedroom closet and reach into my Marble Life jar to retrieve my week's marble, a sense of arousal and pent-up anticipation builds up. I can't tell you if this lasts for a second, as I reach into the jar; or for minutes, as I approach to enter the closet; or when I wake up in the morning and first think about my ritual that is about to unfold. It is a seductive emotion, powered by anticipation, as I go through my very personal and intimate ritual of selecting a marble that will live with me for a week. I am about to start a new chapter in my life . . . and in the life of everyone who comes in contact with me. My emotions run deep.

This week's marble is selected.

Projection = Excitement.

I see the marble. Feel the marble. Roll the marble. Sense the marble. I project or channel onto the marble what I want to accomplish and how I want to spend my moments this week. A wave of excitement takes over as I literally kiss the marble, welcoming it into my life. I embrace the marble and carefully, purposefully, lovingly, consciously place the marble onto my person (into my right-hand pocket.)*

---

* I put the marble in my right-hand pocket where I interact with it throughout the day. A pocket is one place. My place. It can live with you wherever you are. You can wear your marble on a chain close to your heart or on a ring in plain sight. It can sit on a pedestal that lives on your desk. Or your marble can live virtually, through your Marble Life app (free to download), where your weekly marble rests peacefully, purposefully on your mobile/tablet screen to be accessed and appreciated by a simple click or tap. Whether your marble lives in the physical world and/or the virtual one, the power of Marble Life is harnessed deep within you.

Reflection = Introspection.

Throughout the week, I reflect. I introspect. I remain acutely aware that my marble is with me. I sense it. I feel its power, its force, its magnetism, its strength. It's a reminder of what is. I feel its connection to me. I remind myself that I am in control of how I spend my marble . . . and the moments that this daily/weekly marble represents. This process of reflection and introspection is repeated throughout the week and reinforced whenever I take it from my pocket. Or feel it in my mind's pocket. My marble is me. It is an external object powered by my internal light. At night, I rest it on my nightstand . . . and wake up to repeat the process and the ritual again. I reflect on my life and the people and the moments in my life. I think about how I spent my marble—and the moments in the week that remain.

Ejection = My unwillingness to let go.

Toward the end of the week, on my last day, when I know that I have to part with my marble and the moments that that marble represented, I don't harness a sense of power or excitement. Quite the contrary. I feel a sadness. I don't want to let it go. I literally have a sense of anxiety as I look at my marble, that special Marble Life object that I held so close to my heart and my soul. I have an unwillingness to let go of the moment(s). But it's time to reflect. And eject. And reset. Sometimes, between you and me, and depending on my week, I keep my old marble . . . placing it in my left pants pocket, until I can find the appropriate moment to let it go.

Repeat. The emotions start all over again. Anticipation. Excitement. Introspection. My unwillingness to let go. The process begins again—Selection. Projection. Reflection. Ejection. I walk into my bedroom closet to choose another Marble . . . to start yet another meaningful chapter in my unfolding life.

⇌ 5 ⇌

Where Is the Starting Line?

Old age is always 15 years older than you are.

—My mother, Joyce Becker,
quoting Bernard Baruch

IT STARTS WITH A SINGLE MARBLE. This marble can be physical or virtual (Marble Life App available on iTunes and Google Play). But it is your marble that kicks off the journey. Then the process of mindfulness takes root. With every day, with every moment, with every experience, you breathe new meaning and renewed life into your marble.

By setting parameters and establishing weekly objectives, you set the stage and define the layers of your Marble Life experience. You can go simple . . . or delve more deeply into Marble Life.

Marble Life can be tailored to your specific needs and life goals. This fun, smart, simple, profound, robust, moldable Life Appreciation System takes the physical concept of *my* marble experience and transfers it to *your* physical and/or virtual life experience. It can be customized to help you be more mindful and to maximize and appreciate the important moments, and people, in *your* daily life.

It starts with a single marble.

Saturday Morning:
Randomly select a single marble.

Hold it.

Sense it.

Project onto it (*the who you want to be*).

Internalize it.

Pocket it.

Throughout the Week:
Channel it.

Carry it.

Appreciate it.

Remember it.

Implement it.

Represent it.

Friday Night/Saturday Morning:
Toss it. Let it go.

Saturday Morning:

Randomly select another marble. A new chapter begins. With each new marble, you are provided a gift, a fleeting opportunity to better meet your life goals. Better the moment. Attach yourself to the now in your life.

≈

Your Marble Life marble is the opposite of a collectible.
    It is the non-collectible.
You don't save it. You don't collect it.
    You spend it.
You discard it. It has only limited value.
    It lives only in the moment.

≈ 6 ≈

You're Somewhere. Are You Here?
Are You There? Are You Aware?

I WAS TALKING TO MY DEAR OLD FRIEND CATHY, telling her about my new experiment with Marble Life, using the marbles to mark the moments of my life so that I could remember to be in the present. Our conversation was deep and profound. It was meaningful, as our conversations are. She chuckled and said, "Every Thursday morning, I remember to take out the garbage. It's funny. I need the garbage to tell me what day it is. Pretty sad."

Of course, as a wise man once said, "One man's garbage is another man's treasure." Even little reminders, like *trash day*, can help you to become more aware of the moment and of living in the now.

If you're like me (and I hope you are not too much like me, because I'm continually struggling to figure me out), you want to be aware, or mindful. or in the present moment of where you are right now, of your surroundings, of your thoughts, and of the people in your life. But why is "*right now*" so difficult to fully grasp? Why is it so difficult to point our finger to this very moment that we are living? If you think about it, we are always in the now. We should be experts on living in the now, as we have a lot of practice. But being truly aware, or living consciously in this micro-moment we call *now*, is not easy. It certainly never came easily to me. There are too many distractions. Personal distractions. Business transactions. Selfish-me distractions. Day-to-day distractions. I think being in the now takes on a whole new meaning, especially when we shine a light on its newly realized importance. Maybe we need a different approach to recognizing and appreciating the now. Maybe we need to be reminded of what now looks and feels like.

Psychologists, when treating patients, will often teach their patients to be aware or mindful of the moment. Dr. Leslie Becker-Phelps, PhD, psychologist, speaker, and author of *Insecure in Love*, will sometimes guide her patients, and teach professionals to guide their patients, to get in touch with their physical body. For instance, if you allow yourself to become aware of a sensation in your chest, a tickle in your throat, or a churning in your belly, you can then choose to pay attention to that sensation that exists only in this present moment. You can then ask yourself what emotions arise from your awareness of that sensation. In doing this, you have used your inner observation of sensation to hopscotch to the emotions of the moment at hand, rather than those from past experiences or brought on by future worries. By directing awareness to the physical self, you can begin to connect on a deeper, more emotionally present, more meaningful level.

Teachers are often tasked with this lesson, as are spiritual leaders. They all use various tools and methods to teach this very important lesson and life tool of awareness. But I am not a psychologist. I am not a teacher. And I am not a spiritual or religious leader. Nor am I an expert in the field of self-awareness. I'm just me. Like you. I'm a regular guy, living day to day, trying to figure myself out and trying to make the most out of my life and the people and the moments and the experiences that make up my life.

So what does it mean to be aware or mindful? At its root, and according to Jon Kabat-Zinn, recognized expert on mindfulness and creator of the Stress Reduction Clinic and the Center for Mindfulness in Medicine, Health Care, and Society, "Mindfulness is the awareness that arises by paying attention on purpose, in the present moment, and non-judgmentally."

As quoted from the *Chinese Buddhist Encyclopedia,* **"Mindfulness,** or **awareness**, is a spiritual faculty considered to be of great importance in the path to enlightenment according to the teaching of the Buddha. . . . Enlightenment is a state of being in which greed, hatred and delusion have been overcome, abandoned and are absent from the mind. Mindfulness is an attentive awareness of the reality of things (especially in the moment). This faculty becomes a power when it is coupled with a clear comprehension of whatever is taking place.

"The Buddha advocated that one should establish mindfulness in one's day-to-day life, maintaining as much as possible a calm awareness of one's bodily functions, sensations (feelings), objects of consciousness (thoughts and perceptions), and consciousness itself. The practice of mindfulness supports analysis resulting in the arising of wisdom."

Susan Kaiser Greenland, American author of *The Mindful Child* and teacher of Mindful Awareness, defines mindfulness from a "classical mindfulness training perspective" as "to remember, or to check in." According to Greenland, "Mindfulness is a way of looking at life experience. Your inner experience. Your outer experience. And both together without blending the two." At her TEDxStudioCityED conference, and in her "Teaching the ABCs of Attention" lecture, she suggests that "we look at our life experiences with attention, balance and compassion. What are we mindful of when we're mindful of our attention?"

∾

Now that we have a general understanding of what mindfulness means, what can we do to be more mindful? More present? More aware? How can we be more mindful of our actions? Of our thoughts? How can we be more mindful of others? And how can we be more mindful of the moments that bookend our day? Included in the next several chapters are ways that you can bring mindfulness and awareness to each moment while you practice your Marble Life Appreciation System.

ᖴ 7 ᖴ

Get in the Know and in the Now

BEFORE WE TAKE THE PLUNGE into some deeper exercises, I want to share some very simple physical and mental exercises one can do to be more aware, or mindful, to bring you into the now, into this very real moment of time.

Get Lost

One exercise I find soothing is to get lost in what others consider the mundane—the daily chores, routines, and basic activities that envelop our lives. Try peeling a banana. I know, this sounds funny and simplistic. But be conscious of the peeling and of the revealing. It takes only a few seconds but it brings you into the moment. Enjoy the moment. Get lost in it. See the way the banana looks as the peel is pulled back, how it smells. Notice the texture of the peel under your hands and the ripeness of the fruit beneath. Put your full attention on peeling the banana, and be rewarded with the banana.

You can do this exercise with any activity. Try peeling an orange. Cut the grass. Bounce a rubber ball. Watch a goldfish swim. Twirl a piece of string. Watch the snow fall. Peel string cheese. Close your eyes for one full minute and listen. Pick up a crayon, close your eyes, and draw. Listen to music and try it again.

You'll be amazed at the calm these simple exercises will bring. But the beauty is in the action, in the detail, and in the nuance. The very objects that surround us in our lives are the tools that can bring us into the moment, if we can stay aware long enough to get lost in our actions. Get lost. You'll be better because of it.

Years ago, an advertising professor in one of my college classes encouraged us, challenged us, to break out of our daily routines. "Try something new," he would say. Not an easy task, because we tend to find comfort and safety in the routines we establish for ourselves. They're a hiding ground. A safety zone. Routines can be prison bars designed to protect us from the new and the unfamiliar. He suggested that once in a while, maybe once a month, we break out and shake it up. "Today, make a conscious effort to take a different route to work." Instead of a right, turn left. Instead of north, go south. Choose a different path. Enjoy the view. Treat yourself to the sights and sounds of your new environment. Today is a blank canvas. Turn your trip into a journey. By mixing it up, you can add a little adventure into your micro moments. So go ahead; take an unfamiliar route. Try a new flavor. Read something new. Shake up your day. Treat yourself to a micro change in your routine and enjoy the reward that comes along with it. It's a gift ready for you to unwrap.

Sounds Like

Rhythmic, soothing sounds bring us inward. They relax us and glide us into the moment. Loud, dominant sounds jolt us and also bring us inward and into the moment. Hence, the juxtaposition of sound.

The pitter-patter of rain. The rustling of leaves blowing in the wind. The soothing sound of crickets chirping. Birds singing. Waves crashing. A river flowing. A baby breathing. A heart beating. A methodical, meditational chant. Rhythmic sounds are magical and whisk us into a state of calm, into a new reality that can help us to appreciate life.

No need for a sound machine. Just open your ears. Listen beyond the noise. Hear the music of life talking to you and bringing you inward.

The pop! of a balloon. The ring of a bell. The scream of a siren. The smash of a cymbal. Loud, dominant sounds break barriers, pierce our comfort zones, and jolt us from a daydream into a steadfast reality. From the confines of our personal space to the clamoring of a crowd, sound bites can penetrate the calm and get us to where we need to be, in an instant. Go to a football game. Teams huddle, they shout, they clap. There's a siren in that little can that screams people into the moment. There's a chant from the crowd. A buzzer at a game. Different sounds move people in different ways and jolt them into reality.

Repetition is relaxing too, and it can have a calming effect. That's why kids (adults, too) watch television shows repeatedly. It's soothing. The same episode. Over and over again. The same characters. The same story line. Familiarity breeds comfort. We count sheep. It relaxes us, so much so that it can put us to sleep. The bell rings at school. It's not just a bell to ring in the change of periods, but the ring itself is loud and abrupt, serving its purpose to jolt us into the start of our day.

A bell in a motel lobby—you ring it to get someone's attention—tells the man in the lobby, "Hey, I'm here, and I need your attention." A horn in your car, when you lean on it, commands attention. It stops an oncoming driver in his tracks, breaks him out of his foggy daze, and brings him to attention. In an instant, he is in a sobering reality, not quite sure how he got there or where he was just a moment ago.

A baby screams. It captures the attention of its mother. A dog barks. It captures the attention of its owner. You slam the door. It captures the attention of the recipient of that action.

Use sound to get you where you need to go. Pay attention to the pitch. Whether the sounds of your day are soothingly soft or soberingly loud, sounds are powerful tools to bring you into your now and to connect you with your inner self.

Living the Marble Life

Listen to your senses. To the sounds. To the smells. To the experiences of the day that surround us. That engulf us. Take the time to soak it in.

Sound Vibrations

Get lost in the sound of a bell, a singing bowl, a chime, a gong, an Om, a hum, or the rhythmic sound of the wind, the sea, the pitter-patter of the rain. A crackling fire. Just as sounds can transport us into a sense of calm, they can also jolt us back into reality, aligning us more closely with our inner self and on track in our current now.

Sound is a tested tool that can bring children into the moment before starting their school day. In key markets throughout the United States, children's test scores were reportedly low in socially challenging urban markets. By the time these children made it to school, their minds were cluttered with affliction, and their test scores were suffering because of it. They could not clear their minds for learning. An experiment ensued where a bell was rung to start the day. The sound of the bell cleared the mind, opened the mind to learning, and test scores soared as a result. Sound can be a powerful tool to bring us into the Now. What sounds do you hear throughout your day? Listen more closely.

The Sound of Music

I think back a number of years ago to a private, guided tour at the Steinway & Sons music factory in Queens, New York. I was asked to tour the factory and come back with product ideas . . . ideas that would play off of the equity of the famous Steinway name. The tour was fascinating. I learned about veneers and imported woods and the curing process. After the tour, we brainstormed and developed product concepts that could be born from the excess woods that could not be used in a Steinway piano, as the Steinway wood-selection process was so extremely selective. Imagine all of the wood that went through the yearlong process only to get tossed aside because it did not meet their demanding standards. But what if we could turn some of that tossed, otherwise unusable wood into a valuable Steinway-related product? We returned with artist drawings of music stands, metronomes, piano benches, music boxes, and an assortment of other Steinway-related products that we believed loyal customers would welcome and gravitate to. The product selection was unique, innovative, and beautiful. But what impressed me the most during this tour, and had the greatest impact on me, was the sound of Steinway. The actual sounds that accompanied us during our tour. The unexpected sounds. The rhythmic sounds. The important sounds. The sounds of greatness. The sounds of music being built. It was fascinating. And powerful. And humbling. The hammering. The banging. The sanding. The making of music was its own music. I was moved. Perhaps the greatest product (in my very humble opinion), beyond the making of the great Steinway, and beyond the innovative product concepts we developed, was the music track that played so proudly, so methodically, so eloquently, so unassumingly in the background . . . like our own private concert, available only to those of us who opened our ears to listen.

What music do you hear in the background? What happens when you push it into the foreground? What do you hear beyond the obvious? What do you hear that adds shades of color, personality, and meaning to your day? Listen up. There is a concert going on and you have the front row seat!

Relax and Breathe

Obviously, our breath is important. Without it, we could not exist. But there are also simple exercises we can do with our breath, beyond the importance of oxygen intake, that will help us let go of our anxiety, relax, lessen life's tensions, bring us into the present, and connect us with our inner self on a deeper, more personal, more meaningful level.

The simplest of exercises (and it comes naturally), is to just breathe. Let your breathing do the work. Not a heavy or forced breathing. Just natural breath. For this simple exercise, the only tool you need is your breath and a little concentration. Good or bad (breath, that is), you always have it with you, so there are no excuses. You can perform this simple breathing-visualization exercise any time you'd like, wherever you happen to be: on the beach, in your backyard, in your bed in the morning or on your pillow at night, at your desk in the afternoon, or in the elevator traveling to a meeting. For the investment of just a few seconds, this simple breathing exercise can make a difference in your search for calmness, inner peace, and self-awareness and can deliver a sense of freedom and a state of calm, life order, and perspective.

Close your eyes and follow the path of your own breath, paying attention to the rhythmic flow of air, and the true me-ness that is you and only you, as it travels through your body and fills your inner being.

Relax your busy mind, let go of your thoughts, and let your breathing do the talking and your mind and body do the listening. Do this for a few seconds or as long as you can maintain the silence in your thoughts. Once you graduate up to fifteen seconds, then try to go for a minute or more of paying attention to your breathing.

During this time, focus only on your breathing. Focus only on this moment. With each deep breath, feel your breathing. Hear your breathing. Internalize your breathing. With each breath you take in, and each breath you let out, focus only on your breath. Follow its path.

It takes a little practice to keep everything out (of your head that is) and to pull yourself in, but once you start to master it, you'll find it easier to do each time. This exercise follows the notion that your breath is grounded in movement, and, if you relax and become mindful of your breathing, you'll slow down just long enough to feel restful. Go ahead—catch your breath. Breathe in. Breathe out. Ride the wave. Journey inside yourself. You will discover a sense of calm, a renewed awareness, and an inner connection. It's a relaxing exercise that is quite powerful. And simple. You don't even need a gym membership to participate.

A Pocket Full of Stuff

Did you ever take the time to notice little children and how playful and intense they are? Take a closer look. There is a lot we can learn by watching our little people play. And laugh. And discover. They are profound teachers enjoying the bliss of unpolluted interaction. Their play is pure. Intense. Joyful. Many children, at the end of the day, have pockets bulging with stuff. Not just any stuff. Important stuff that they collected throughout their day's journey. Stuff that meant something to them. It is a ball or a pebble or a stamp or a twig or a spider or a leaf or whatever it was that resonated with them at that time. Kids like to carry things in their pockets and reflect on them.

As adults, we carry things more in our "mental pockets" than our physical ones—it could be something someone said that was hurtful or the instance when you were cut off in traffic. It could be a compliment on your new wardrobe or the excitement you felt over the fact that it's Friday afternoon, going into a long weekend! It could be that you have not lived up to the life goals you have set for yourself, that you have misappropriated your day, or that you let the little moments that matter slip by. These things in our "mental pockets" are just as important as the actual stuff that kids carry around and need to be taken out every once in a while as well.

Allow yourself to show your pocket stuff to a friend, a family member, a confidant, or even just write it down in your journal. Getting these things out of your mental space and into physical space (vocal or written) will free up your pockets and leave you feeling lighter and more aware of what affected you throughout your day.

What do you carry in your *"pocket"* to reflect on your day's journey?

➣ 8 ➢

We Hear, but We Don't Listen

I Can't Hear You, I Have My Head in My Ear!

We DON'T GET A LOT OUT OF OUR DAY, because we don't pay attention to the details, to the individual moments that make up our day. We coast. It's only human. We go from one routine to another routine to another. Before we know it, our day rolls into night, and we don't know how we got there. We barely remember where we spent the moments that made up our day. What a waste of precious time.

It is difficult to be mindful when we don't pay attention to what we should be mindful of.

You can argue all you want. But it's true. Try a little experiment: Spend one day this week and pay attention. Really pay attention. Do a little less talking and a little more listening. Soak in your surroundings.

During this little experiment, ask someone how they are doing. Put aside the little conversations that are going on inside your head and really listen to them (not you). Look at them. Really look at them. Study them. Look into their eyes. What color are their eyes? Look into their soul. What do you see? Notice their mouth moving. Watch them talk. Pay attention to their mannerisms. Really listen to their words, to what they are saying to you.

Several things will happen within the span of this encounter. First, you will get more out of the conversation. You will get more out of that moment, and you will really learn something about yourself, about the person you are talking to, and about the subject matter at hand. The person you are talking to will connect with you on a deeper level. You will have a true, meaningful connection. They will remember you. You are asking someone how they are, and now you are genuinely listening to their answer. You're giving yourself to them by truly listening. But guess what? In a strange way, you're being selfish because you will quickly learn that you feel better about yourself in the process. You have enriched the conversation and touched a person's life. It was meaningful. You were in the now. And you brought them along for the ride. You were really listening to what was happening in that moment. You paid attention. And you are better because of it. The day will pass and you will remember that moment because you lived that moment.

Years ago, the great Harry Lorayne, a frequent guest of the also-great Johnny Carson, would walk out on stage at the start of *The Tonight Show*. Harry would ask everyone in the audience to stand. He would proceed to walk into the audience, face to face with each guest, and ask their name. Upon spurting their name, that guest would sit down as Harry would proceed to the next guest. Again he would ask their name, they would tell him and proceed to sit down. After many guests, the audience would be seated. Johnny would interview Harry, go to commercial break, and return to finish the show. At the end of *The Tonight Show*, Harry did something remarkable. He would ask the entire audience to stand. Harry walked into the audience, pointed at each person, and repeated them their name back to them. One by one, they would sit down. This continued until every guest would hear Harry tell them their name. I bought Harry Lorayne's book, *Remembering People*, to learn the trick. Guess what? There was no trick. The fact is, we don't remember people's names because we never really hear their name in the first place. Take the time to listen. Repeat what you hear. With a little practice, you'll pay closer attention to the moment and to the people who interact with you.

❧ 9 ❧

Math Your Day

IF YOU DON'T BELIEVE THAT TIME is fleeting, or if you think you're filling your days up fully, consider doing the math to find where the time goes in your average day. The following numbers come from the US Department of Labor's statistics regarding time spent in primary activities for the civilian population eighteen years and over, and represent the national average for 2013. Your personal statistics will likely differ, so do the math for yourself, and see where you come in!

There are twenty-four hours in a day. We spend:

- 9.36 hours on personal-care activities (8.6 hours just sleeping)

- 1.16 hours eating and drinking

- 1.85 hours on household activities (housework, food prep, cleanup, lawn, garden)

- .73 hours purchasing goods and services

- 1.42 hours caring for and helping household members

- .12 hours caring and helping nonhousehold members

- 4.20 hours working and on work-related activities

- .25 hours with educational activities (attending class, homework, research)

- .31 hours on organizational, civic, religious, and spiritual activities

- 4.17 hours on leisure and sports activities (socializing, communicating, TV/online, sports, exercise)

- .11 hours on telephone, mail, and email

- And .31 on other activities

This leaves us with exactly .01 hours remaining.

With nearly all of our time spoken for, it is essential that we pay attention to each moment as it arises and use it to its fullest advantage. In order to create awareness for the present moment, consider the following questions, and see what answers come up for you:

- How do you spend your moments?

- Are you getting the most out of your day and out of every moment?

- On a scale of 1–10, how would someone you love rate the busy-ness of your day?

- On a scale of 1–10, how would you rate yourself?

- Are you paying attention to what is important in your life?

- If not, what can you change to use your moments, minutes, and hours more wisely?

≈ 10 ≈

Look at Yourself: Take Note

IF YOU FIND YOURSELF WITH A POOR RATING left over from the previous chapter or have discovered that you're not putting your attention on the things that matter most, the following exercises can help you pay attention to what is important in your life and help you to map your day and your life journey.

Exercise 1: Take pen to paper. It can draw you in. Write out your day by the hour. Start with Monday and work your way through Sunday. Now look at your hourly breakout and ask yourself, "Am I spending my time wisely? Productively? Lovingly? Am I living my day? Am I investing in my moments? Am I paying attention to what is important in my life today?" Now grab a pen and a new sheet of paper. Change one hourly entry each day this week. Rewrite your life course. Delete one ho-hum hourly entry that just is and replace that one entry with a more productive entry that will get you closer to what you want.

Exercise 2: Draw your personal clock. One big circle. Write in an average core activity within each hour block.

What does your clock tell you? Does it paint a picture of your daily life and how you spend your moments? Do your daily objectives support your life objectives? Your today objectives? Are you rolling today's *Didn't Get To* into tomorrow's *Must Do*? Are you running out of day? Are you spending quality time with those you love or care about? How are you spending your moments? Your minutes. Your hours. What can you do to remind yourself that your moments matter and that you are in control of your life and the moments that make up your life? You control your clock. Make your minutes count.

Now delete one hour block, one core activity, from your clock. Erase it. Which core activity would you take away? By removing one core activity, you place more emphasis on the hour blocks (the core activities) that remain. Pull away what's less important in your day, and place your focus on what really matters in your quest for a better day and a more meaningful you.

Now delete another hour block. Which core activity is deleted? Which hour blocks remain? Are you seeing your day more clearly? Are the core activities that remain representative of what you want out of your day? Out of your life? Your clock is ticking. It's time to make each tick count.

Another thing you can do is to create a separate clock, and this time fill the hour blocks with the activities you want to undertake. Maybe you'll replace "TV time" with "family time" or "gym time." Swap out "bring dinner home" for "cook dinner with the whole family." Even changing just an hour in the daily routine can bring a new awareness to every moment.

Exercise 3: Cut it out! Go to a magazine or to Google Images and spend some time cutting out or printing photos illustrating the life you see for yourself. Take those photos and place them on a sheet of paper, with your photo smack in the center. Take a photo of your new life collage and carry that photo with you as a visual reminder of how you want to spend your moments to secure the life you want. Remember, it is never too late to update your life collage. As Napoleon Hill once said, "Whatever the mind of man can conceive and believe, it can achieve."

≈ 11 ≈

Slip into the Moment

Music to Your Ears

I stumbled upon a wonderful little experience that I would like to share with you. Running to the gym early one morning, I couldn't seem to find my music player. So I grabbed my daughter's little pink iPod Nano, along with her white earbuds, and headed to the gym. At the start of my routine, I placed the earbuds into my ears, hit shuffle, then play. My workout began. Without realizing it, and within fifteen minutes into my program, it occurred to me that I was listening to what my daughter listens to. There was no narration, no preamble, no edits. Just her music in my ears. I knew I had stumbled onto something special. My workout continued. So did my special bond with my daughter. I continued playing her Nano in my head throughout the course of the week. It was fascinating, innocent, and organic. I felt a closeness with her that I had never experienced before.

Borrow your child's digital music player (i.e., iPod, Walkman, MP3, etc.). Now listen to it. It's like peeking into their soul. Borrow your daughter's digital player and listen to it during your routine today (at the gym, on a walk). You'll be awakened. You'll listen to the lyrics in a way you never did before, as the lyrics are foreign to you but familiar to her. You'll hear what she hears. You'll be in her ear. You'll be awakened. Now borrow your son's music player. Walk in his shoes. Tap to his beat.

Do you really know your friend? Your neighbor? Your mother? Ask to borrow your friend's iPod or music player. And give them yours. Expose yourself. You know that your neighbor is a banker. Listen to his playlist. Does he "sound" like a banker? Or an ice cream store owner? Or a screenwriter? Or the outer shell of a person you thought you knew, but didn't? You may be surprised and enlightened and pleased with what you learn. With what you hear.

The only caveat is that you must ask to borrow their player without any warning. You don't want them to clean it up or alter their playlist in any way. And borrow it for a minimum of three days. Put it on shuffle. Listen and learn. Something caused them to add that song or entry to their playlist, at one time or another in their life. What you hear will be music to your ears.

It's important to truly get to know the people around you, to look at the world through their eyes—especially the eyes of your closest loved ones. In order to appreciate them, and your moments with them, you will need to get to know them first.

As I mentioned before, I was thirty-eight when I lost my dad. A concept that was impossible for me to understand. How could all of that energy, that knowledge, that intellect, that belief system, that mind, that structure of a man, that father, that son, that husband, that brother, that soul, just end? How is that possible? Is that even possible? He lives in my heart. The shame of it, though, is that I never really got to know my father . . . beyond him being my father. Who was he? Why did I never really understand him? Is it that he died too young? That he never opened up to me? Or that we never sat down and talked and got to really know one another? I wish he were still alive. What would he tell me today? I'm a different person now. I'm older. Wiser. More receptive. I would take the time to know him. And appreciate him. Of course, we can't go back. We can, however, make this moment count and turn today into a more meaningful experience.

∾

How well do you know your family?

How well do they know you?

How well do you know you?

Who are the important people in your life?

Why are they important?

What would you say to them if you were given the chance?

You are given the chance.

∾

Each moment that we cherish in our lives, each *marble*, comes not just from what we did, but whom we shared those moments with. If we learn from others, and in turn expose ourselves, we can learn to live beyond the regrets of "I never knew who they really were." I wish I had a chance to listen to my own father's iPod and to experience his music through his ears, as I know I would have gained a deeper understanding and appreciation of him and his role in my life.

Pinch Me

Both my daughter and son play lacrosse. They've played the game from elementary school to high school to traveling lacrosse to college. I don't know much about the game. Everything I've learned, I've learned from watching them play. But I do know one thing. As I have often told my daughter, *"Just because you are on the field doesn't mean you are in the game."* Get in the game. Be in the game.

I've shared a little trick with my daughter that I will now share with you. If you need to bring yourself into the game, right now, this instant, pinch yourself. Literally— pinch your ear. It is an instant reminder, a jolt to the system that you need to get current. That you need to get in the game. Right now! That you need to break out of your daze, out of the ho-hum of your routine, and remind yourself that you're here.

It works. Try it. Pinch yourself and get in the game. You'll be better because of it.

There's the old story of the man who walked around with a rock in his shoe. That little pebble reminded him, every second, that he was in the present moment. I like to think of the Pinch-Me Trick as a little shoe pebble, one that pipes up to say, "Hey! Put your focus here, in the now, where it belongs."

Talk to a Candle

Many religions incorporate practices of using candles to talk to the dead, like a Yizkor candle in the Jewish religion, used in the prayer for the departed. In Hebrew, *Yizkor* means "remember." During a Yizkor prayer, we remember the souls of our relatives, loved ones, and closest friends. When we light a Yizkor candle, we renew and strengthen the connection between us and our lost ones.

We light this little white candle to commemorate the lives of our loved ones and to reflect on their memory. Once lit, its flame dances around, casts a flickering shadow, and throws off a swath of warmth that triggers emotion and somehow encases our inner conversations into an enveloping memory and a live enactment of what once was. One little flame. One powerful candle.

Across faiths, candles play a religious and/or celebratory role. Votive candles, or prayer candles, are often displayed in Roman Catholic churches. Brass *diyas* are permanent fixtures in homes and temples. Diyas are native to India and are often used in Hindu and Sikh religious festivals. A similar lamp called a butter lamp is used in Tibetan Buddhist offerings as well. The candle has extended beyond religious and spiritual rituals to the curative powers of aromatherapy and the symbolic harmony of color theory. And then, of course, there is the birthday candle.

Birthday candles are blown out in celebration of the moment, often accompanied by song. Yizkor candles are never blown out, burning slowly, uninterrupted, often accompanied by prayer or words of love. Whether it's a Yizkor candle to memorialize the dead or a birthday candle to celebrate the living, the alluring properties of a candle can transport us to a place deep within ourselves. Talking to a candle can bring what is harnessed deep inside of us outside. It can help us to break through our outer walls and talk to ourselves in a way that penetrates and permeates.

So whether it's a Yizkor candle, a votive or prayer candle, a diya, a butter lamp, a common candle, or a birthday candle, through the mesmerizing flicker of a small flame, you can experience and internalize the power of meditational fire and the enlightenment that it can cast into our lives.

My favorite part about communicating with a candle is that, by its very nature, the candle is changing in the moment. The flame dances and changes, flickering and flaring, and it is never the same flame twice. When I speak to the candle, my breath moves the flame, a reminder to stay in the moment, to watch the candle as it is, and to pay attention to my own emotions and to be completely present.

If I am grieving or celebrating, or simply want to talk, being in the moment is essential for me to connect to my emotions. I can watch the candle and know that in this moment I am sitting in a heart-to-heart communication with myself or my loved one who has already passed. This allows me to process my words and feelings as they arise in a way that my conscious mind may have trouble processing.

Go ahead. Turn down a light. Light up a candle. Let the flame lead the way. Relax. Feel the flame on your face (not too close). Get lost in the motion. In the flicker. In yourself. Get close and personal. Watch the flame dance to your breath and react to your voice. Your words will flicker inward.

Old World and New World Techniques—Qigong

I was talking to my friend Dan. He comes from a different cultural background from mine. We were deep in conversation about life and philosophy and Asian culture and the things we do, or try to do, to help us to appreciate the moment and identify the now—our now. He shared with me an exercise he performs daily. It is called Qigong. This mind-over-matter exercise was passed down to him by his father—and his father's father before him. I found it fascinating.

Throughout the ages, people from different cultures and from around the globe have incorporated mental, physical, and meditational exercises into their daily lives, learning from the generation(s) before them, exercising practices that have provided an easily accessible life tool to self-cultivate, strengthen their mind, and heal their bodies. One such practice, with roots in Chinese medicine, and as explained to me by Dan, is Qigong. According to the National Qigong Association, "The word Qigong (Chi Kung) is made up of two Chinese words. Qi is pronounced *chee* and is usually translated to mean the life force or vital energy that flows through all things in the universe. The second word, Gong, pronounced, *gung*, means accomplishment, or skill that is cultivated through steady practice. Together, Qigong means cultivating energy. Qigong is an integration of physical postures, breathing techniques, and focused intentions. People do Qigong to maintain health, heal their bodies, and calm their minds. When aspects of Qigong are integrated, it encourages a positive outlook on life, creates a balanced lifestyle, and brings greater harmony, stability, and enjoyment into everything we do." While there is a wide variety of practices, exercises, and variations to Qigong, as it is an ancient art form that could fill many books, one such Qigong practice, as passed along to me from Dan, is to hold a small log, or stick, in a meditative posture and to clear the mind. Then meditate and concentrate on the stick and mark the stick with a notch, or a number, every day for 100 days.

Each and every day, you focus on the stick, you focus on the notch, you focus on the now. Each day you bring in the new and layer it on top of the now. After 100 days of looking within, of introspection, you've grown and learned to appreciate each day, each notch of life.

When beginners ask, "What is the most important aspect of practicing Qigong?" the answer is . . . "*just do it.*"

There is a clear correlation, a parallel, between projecting onto a stick and projecting onto a marble. Both illustrate the similarities of projection channeling onto an object and the meditative, or healing, benefits of doing so.

☞ 12 ☜

The Now You

I HAVE ALWAYS BEEN KEENLY AWARE and a distant, guarded observer of self-help books and audiotapes and motivational speakers. While there is power in those, and a thirst for them, the real power comes from within, as communicated in Napoleon Hill's *Think and Grow Rich* (which I devoured when I was ten years old—my favorite chapter was "Three Feet from Gold") to Transcendental Meditation (TM), to *The Power of Now*, to the teachings of Tony Robbins, to Rhonda Byrne's *The Secret*. While I have observed from afar and have immersed myself in many great readings from many great teachers, I've always preferred to reach deep within myself to stir up the motivation and the change that needed changing. After all, we have to find within ourselves our desire and willingness to change. Only then can change take form.

It's one thing to "hear" what we should do. It's another to "do" what we should do. As Benjamin Franklin so eloquently stated, "Well done is better than well said."

My suggestion is to keep on reading. Keep on listening. Keep on learning. Keep on pushing. And keep on reminding ourselves of the person we want to be and the steps we need to take to get there. It's a process.

Marble Life can serve as a powerful daily reminder, a mechanism, a projection channeling tool, to help us to pay attention to this moment, to channel our thoughts inward, and to work on our ever-changing "changing" that needs changing.

Every day we are at a crossroad. Today, make Marble Life your own. Enjoy what you have. Pay attention. Your marble is you.

Get to know the real you. Get to know your father. Get to know your children. Get to know everyone who matters in your life. Let them in. Spend quality time with your loved ones. Put the focus on what is important. Take the time to pay attention to what is happening right now. Look around. Listen. Take a micro view. Immerse yourself. Challenge yourself. Free yourself. Enjoy the day. Enjoy your moment.

We spend so much time worrying about tomorrow, so little time appreciating today.

Appreciate today!

—David G. Becker

Marble Life Credo

Today will pass. As will tomorrow. And every day after that. So you can approach each day with vigor or you can let each day slide by.

This very second is all you have. It rolls into a minute, which rolls into an hour, which rolls into your day. Your day folds into a week. Your week into a month. Your month into a year. The year timelines into your life. But how do you choose to live your life? Those seconds. Those minutes. Those hours. Those days. Those weeks. Those years that define your body of life?

Your life is a succession and a culmination of moments and the experiences of those moments. Today is all you have. This minute, made up of seconds clicking away. Each minute that comes is a minute that goes. Time is fleeting. Every second counts. Every moment matters.

Today is right in front of you. Staring you down. You have this minute to spend as you see fit. Not as others see fit. This is your minute. Your moment. Your life. How you choose to spend your minute is entirely up to you. Spend it wisely. Spend it foolishly. But spend it. Today is your day. It belongs to you and you only. How you choose to spend your minute, and the minutes that make up your day, and ultimately your life, will define you and may very well shape or influence all those you touch. So spend today like you mean it. Like it matters. Because it does. Today, do. Undo. Try. Listen. Experiment. Explore. Invent. Expose. Fail. Laugh. Play. Cry. Learn. Love. Give.

Today belongs to you.

Bibliography

The majority of this book, its essence, was drawn from the author's personal experiences and observations over many years of participating in the Marble Life exercise. The author has also made liberal use of concepts introduced and reported on by thought leaders in the fields of meditation, motivation, Zen Buddhism, and mindfulness. I thank them for their inspiration and dedication to their respective fields.

Byrne, Rhonda. *The Secret*, audiobook. New York: Simon and Schuster Audio, TS Production, 2006.

Davis, Jeffrey. *1,000 Marbles: A Little Something about Precious Time*. Kansas City, MO: Andrews McMeel Publishing, 2001.

Hill, Napoleon. *Think and Grow Rich*. Meriden, CN: The Ralston Society, 1937.

Tolle, Eckhart. *The Power of Now: A Guide to Spiritual Enlightenment*. Vancouver, BC, Canada: Namaste Publishing, 1999.

Resources

To learn more about Marble Life® and My Life Appreciation System®, visit www.marble-life.com or download the free Marble Life® app at the App Store or Google Play.

About the Author

Denise Vannucci

David Becker is the president and founder of Blue Plate Media Services, a global media strategy, planning, and buying agency. He has written numerous articles on advertising, marketing, and media strategy and is a frequent speaker on consumer marketing. As an industry advocate for small and mid-sized companies navigating the shifting media landscape, he has guided over one hundred companies in launching new consumer products across North America. A recipient of New York's "Young Entrepreneur of the Year," David has successfully launched multiple businesses over the past thirty years and has invented, imported, and marketed consumer products for major retailers including Target, Federated Stores, and QVC.

David lives in Summit, New Jersey, with his wife, two children, and two dogs. He lives his life one marble at a time.

www.ingramcontent.com/pod-product-compliance
Lightning Source LLC
Chambersburg PA
CBHW031948070426

42453CB00006BA/313